The Hunted River

Robert S. King

FutureCycle Press
www.futurecycle.org

The original edition of this work was published in 2009 by Shared Roads Press, which has graciously given permission for us to republish it in a second edition, with minor changes.

Published by FutureCycle Press
Mineral Bluff, Georgia, U.S.A.

ISBN 978-0-9839985-5-6

for all who never feel at home

Contents

Part 1.
Go the Way of Dreams

The Juggler Tells His Children of Dreams...9
Treasure Hunt...10
Ice-Sparkles...11
Wanting to Write Songs.. 12
A Loiterer's Diary.. 13
When All Is Said and Done..14
Prophets Climbing to Machu Picchu... 15

Part 2.
Go the Way of Memory

Fading Pictures..19
The New World Dictionary...20
Punctuation...21
Going Through the Motions...22
The Meaning of Dogs... 23
What Missing the Cat Means.. 24
Habits and Children in Our Old Age..25
Legacy...26
The Light Sedative of Dark...27

Part 3.
Go the Way of Labor

The Glass Heart..31
Veterans Know a Purr Is Just an Infant Growl.......................................32
Confessions of the Slower Sprinter..33
The Scarecrow at Harvest Time...34
In the Palms of Our Hands..35
Mirror at the Speed of Light... 36
Primal TV...37
Why I Bought a Truck..38
Men.. 39
The Gentleman Who Woke Up as a Goat... 40
Going-Away Party...41
Sculpting the Desert..42

Part 4.
Go the Way of Land

Sanctuary...45
Rock Road..46
Duality...47
Motions... 48
Regret...50
The Last Supper Date...51
Direction...52
Road Steam.. 53
Daydreaming at Rush Hour..54
Miniverse, My Universe... 55
Into Some Deeper Night... 56
Earthen Well.. 57
Ice Steeples, Road Signs... 58

Part 5.
Go the Way of Water

Progress... 61
River Pulse... 62
Lighthouse.. 63
Cottonmouth Catchers in a Night Swamp...............................64
The Underground River... 65
Dream of the Electric Eel.. 66
Knots... 67
The Treasure of Bone.. 68
The Hunted River.. 69
Passing Through.. 73

Part 6.
Go the Way of Wind

The Wind Is Often Sudden Here.. 77
Weeding the National Harvest... 78
The Last Saint of the Empire... 79
Faith.. 80
Windfall..81
How Trees Travel.. 82
Relativity.. 83

Acknowledgments..85

Part 1.
Go the Way of Dreams

The Juggler Tells His Children of Dreams

wear no hard wedding bands
when juggling eggs
let the hands be a clock
circling with the softness of patience

what is falling free
will hatch in a nest of wind
soon you will toss up birds

Treasure Hunt

When the moon hatches
and a million egrets drift down as snow,
when shell bits glow for a moment at our feet,
we'll ask the black and white sky,
is the earth an egg we blossom from
or one we've sat on too long?

And those who've never flown, the trees,
will seem to answer in the chatter of leaves
flying off on wind's will as flocks of kites,
and something, be it death or attitude,
will blow us off our feet,

drag us along just off the earth,
thick with night and its heartbeats,
the broken egg of us a wing above
the glowing ivories of our bones.

Ice-Sparkles

Tonight all lovers bow their drunken heads:
balls of crystal light orbit the bottom of a pond.
Lairs and nests purr submerged between stones.
Across a universe of tongues, the Loch Ness and fawn
together lap ancient water from the pool in our hands.

Between our eyes the stars hang on chandeliers.
Bold in this looking glass, the wet moon
swells to face a night of eyes.
Here we are born of falling ice,
and wed of rising flame, our smoke
making ghosts out of love.

Wanting to Write Songs

when the bad songs of another
are too loud in your room
and yet you linger in their tune

when the trains you never caught
shudder under your bed
and the windows are off key with the wind

then will you feel that silent mockingbird
swelling in your throat
then will you shake the sheet and rise
to the deaf mute you've combed in the mirror

to hear the wind whistle in your hair
and fill your lungs with song

A Loiterer's Diary

A long life of needles no longer stings.
The past no longer stabs in the back.
The future has no sharp point.
The streets I live on have no sharp turns.

The hard sidewalks feel only my lowering weight.
Like snow powder, I'm slowly blowing away;
or kicked like a can, the wind scolds
my metal tumble away, where among the skyscraper
tombstones no one hears a loiterer's clang of cup,
and no Thanksgiving diners hear the wild
outside their warm, foggy windows.

I no longer pity myself in the street puddle mirror.
I'm past recognition, past time, past unheard pleas
only halfway out of my mouth.
Seldom now do these hands stray from my lukewarm breath,
from my blood-warm, empty pockets.
Words medicate themselves.
Sorrow is just another word for sedative.
Soul is another word for shadow.
Love is a whisper behind closed doors.

Only this bum leg still swells with pride,
as useful as a crippled wing dragging
a ragged life behind it, leaving a trail, a guide
to how hope is a stale trail of breadcrumbs,
how life as a shadow no longer feels cold,
how the deepest night blankets my shivers,
tucks in my stone-cold, invisible dreams.

When All Is Said and Done

Tonight all voices join their own echoes.
Broadcast towers curl into question marks.
Horn honks die down into a deep listening.
Traffic stalls at sewer holes, manholes,
spinning wormholes sucking in the city lights.

Everything but silence has been said.
All is lost but everywhere is near.
Flowers and flesh turn a shade of gray.
Millions forget their native tongues,
drop their titles and mirrors,
see now the cost of living,
the cost of not living.

Above skyscrapers a smog lifts, a skin sheds.
A vision light years long comes back.
Stars shoot through the rear-view mirrors,
through the windows rippling like water.
And whether we look up or down,
Andromeda joins our Milky Way, stirs our atoms,
our souls, into a single point of light.

Prophets Climbing to Machu Picchu

a séance blows from lower nights
and we glance back to flickering jewels
to see our eyes lying
like old stones
we lift them from our brother's grave

hurl them ahead to crown a silent mountain
hear them landing in a better time to wear them
    but they never settle they remember
    us falling
    us climbing the path with stones in our pockets
    brother brother step aside throw faster
    our eyes are rolling back to us

Part 2.
Go the Way of Memory

Fading Pictures

A leaf on the ground turns
to powder in the wind
as your sister spirit leaves.
Still you hear her everywhere,
in the door hinge that cries
or squeals her joy
a little less loudly each day.

They'll never fully fade,
these pictures where you find her again.
And you touch her again
in hair tangled in the brush,
in small depressions on the cushions,
in the dark when you brush
against her scented pillow
or hear the tap-walk of her feet
a little less loudly each night.

Her absence is a presence,
a breath you can never quite exhale.

The New World Dictionary

Every word I've said has taken root,
grows the definitions of me—wildflower or wildfire—
smokes from truth's fiercest battle
from whose barrel the best of me blooms,
or remains a scent, a possibility, a whisper
as leaf-rustle in a flock of thrashers
who know how they change color
before the fall.

Every word I've said has been uprooted,
a forget-me-not given rain but no light,
given to the wind of God's conscience,
around the small world
blowing things together, apart.

The same word wages war as powers peace:
desire, the stem of fire and flower.

Punctuation

Am I the point I make of myself?
A million question marks have bent double
into final periods, into black holes on dead-end roads.
I sit in the bottom's rock of ages, a pendulum
rocking chair torn between the tenses.
Cobwebs weave my fingers together;
I breathe but little now when I tilt forward,
choke when I fall back.

If I could edit my life as this line I shape,
not to see my age empty beyond the colon:
Listen to my silence. It dots the eye very well
and will see your plans ricocheting on the same road,
and though your pen learns proper punctuation,
you, like my proper noun, in your life sentence,
may have the one fatal subject-verb disagreement,
where *I* and *am* invert.

Going Through the Motions

Still I mow the face grass every morning,
bathe all my private parts,
make coffee stronger than I am.

Still I work and work and work . . .
though nothing really seems to work,
no matter how hard I punch the clock..

I seem always outside my body:
The shadow of my shadow,
my daydream drives me home.

Tonight I heat the last frozen diet
you left behind,
toss in half-sleep, flicker-light,
heartburn, and dream rags.

And between shades of meaning
I grope for a photograph, a letter,
a familiar scent, *anything*
that would have made you stay.

The Meaning of Dogs

The trail of a young dog is old,
comes back to me as my son
rolling in wagging stalks of grass and tail,
a trick new as the judgeless tongue
wetting him with laughter.

I want to grow
only from remembered grass,
want to part its secrets
with gentle wind, want
my son to sing without
my howl of history.
I do not want this leash
that jerks me back in line,
makes me hold my tongue
on pet words I should not choke on.

What Missing the Cat Means

—for Ian, my son, after Thai went away

It means that something in nature hungered for change,
perhaps the cat, maybe his taker,
perhaps the circular soul of give and take, life and death.

Loss is a hole that forget-me-nots grow back around.
Loyalty is a beautiful gown of leaves
worn together for a season.
Then the pet will not so much leave you as go on.
Or change his form, invisible as wind
that blows far beyond a mere nine lives.

We sweep the floor where his shed white fur
almost forms him whole again.
He is still in our gravity
in the snake's or the hawk's eye.
His taker has taken on his white shadow,
his night vision, and among the crickets
his purr and soft rubbings.

You will always have him,
though you must seek him beyond this moment's void.
Keep his touch to warm your room
but look out across these whiskers of grass,
let him hunt there in a greater self.
Love that holds is less than love that frees,
but you may keep the gift
of knowing that whatever his form,
he's moved by your gentle rain, still feels
your hands softly along his rainbowed back.

Habits and Children in Our Old Age

Our small dog downstairs demands her biscuit,
barks a five p.m. ritual of royalty,
striking like a clock that cannot stop.

In dog years she's my bitchy senior,
but we're both hungry and set in our same old ways.
We both know my walking cane
will carefully poke each stair, each day,

down slowly to her barking dance,
her majesty's long toenails
tap dancing on the kitchen tile,
her chihuahua opera almost shattering windows,
her fat tail ticking to scold me of neglected duty.

After long journey, I wag my tongue in lecture—
"you want your damn biscuit?"—
and swallow my own daily bitter pill.

I toss her a bone off the wall; this biscuit bounce
hits her mouth but never the floor.
It is familiar flavor, magical as catnip,
a sedative to Queen Bitch,
a nursery rhyme for long-forgotten puppy dreams,

until my wife and I sit down to leftovers,
setting off some rote alarm clock,
some scream of ancient hunger
the dog will grumble to the bitter end.

I'll recall then what a good boy was I,
sour and barking at my mother
for candy until she made me sweet again.

Legacy

I die with the last to remember me,
or perhaps with the first
burning an old picture no one can name,
or maybe with these undeciphered words
centuries hence when my language is dead.

No, I do not die here beneath a cold, electric moon,
not in these tubes that tangle me,
not in someone else's blood pumping in me.
My death will be a light in yours
put out some other moonless night.

I'll have no biographer, just a strong will
whose lifeline tied together, burned into
a night sky of minds, of memories
one by one blinking out.

To you who one night alone
carries the last dim torch for me,
who to my vanity will be the last person on earth,
please listen to an old wind in the flickerlight,
whispering to your death ear perhaps just goodbye,
perhaps my last name.

The Light Sedative of Dark

The measured clap clap of my teaspoon on the table
awaiting my dose and the do-not-drive warnings
to easy-chair me into re-runs and the dim hum
of test patterns, multiple choice game shows
with each answer wrong, innovative boredom,
black and white documentaries on the private lines of aging,
indecipherable waves on cables and satellites
whirring on their wrinkling orbits.

So I give myself to the gray light of sleep,
my dream on its back like a crocodile luxurious to
the tummy-rubbing therapeutic masseuse.

I remember before we are born we say goodbye,
hold our noses and dive into this cold medicine called breath.
The sun turns us darker all our lives.
We look for rhyme and find but one,
womb and tomb,
the only rift between them a waiting room.

Part 3.
Go the Way of Labor

The Glass Heart

there is a man so much for love
that he keeps it in a safe
for there have been pink stones at his window
there have been hard slaps at his door
and through the woods she sings so high
in the pitch-dark night

Veterans Know a Purr Is Just an Infant Growl

War is my wife; Peace my tortured child.
The jungle maneuvers around me:
flashlights, flashbacks, growls, and whistles.
At a far distance from myself,
I have grown close to my enemies, their lover now,
have sharpened their claws and stood in a scented wind.
Now in domestication, my animals cry to be fed,
and there is always a girl who listens too hard.

Too easy, your arms bend easy.
Your prayer goes off with the lamp.
You brush against my hands like a generous cat
the color of night, the color of love.
Then you rise purring and
rub your way down the hall to doors with no knobs.
I know I'll take another of your dwindling lives,
as I smoke with a waiting grin
in the room where light jams under the door.

Now I remember the night air licking its wounds,
strong men weeping in a hollow tree,
the silence in rain when the shouts have moved on.
Then silence stretching to find a voice:
light alarmed in the distant sky,
headless turtles cowering under helmets,
fingers planted in fields like carrots.

I want two throats,
one to strangle, one to sing.
I want you to wag your tail,
bite it off,
and blame me.

Confessions of the Slower Sprinter

Always my feet are a split second behind my heart,
almost winners. My chest is nearly
thick enough to reach the tape
and snap it louder than the gun.
Imagine me wearing the magic number,
running toward the award of a woman
who would change her name for me.

For the first time I see more than your back,
its number one stuck out like a finger,
or an old lecture, or a sign that says
stop do not pass. Now I hear
for the first time your soles sucking
behind me, taking deeper and slower
breaths through their rubber lips,
twisting your muscle into silence.

Then my lungs gather a second wind of pride;
the wind behind me spins you around.
My chest swells towards the tape
to measure itself in the volume of cheers
The first failure of your feet does not slow me down.
I run past smeared applause and the blindness of cameras,
towards rehearsed modesty and trophetic gleamings.
I run to make speeches with my head bowed
in your shadow, to praise you and take your cup, saying,
"He who is weighted with trophies
does not run as fast."
I drink ice water from a trophy already engraved
with your name, a prize now full of my lips,
as I freeze the thought that, when you passed me,
you slipped on my sweat.

The Scarecrow at Harvest Time

while crows black as ash
nibble the ears of scarecrows
you recline in the garden
with lips as wet as morning soil

I guard your late gardens
your two pumpkins riper since midnight
are frosted with flaky dew:
Cinderella's dandruff if the truth were known

your fingers snake along my boneless back
the shrinking Prince once most erect of all men
has lost his sword in battle
now in his new passions
what is not soft is numb

this is the only time I'm on top:
your back is soiled by the black dirt
your shed gown lies in the path of melting pumpkins
and you are here to touch my straw lips to yours
shoo the loud crows
who have flown off with parts of me
to build their nests

how many times have you untacked me from the post
to be the sound of a straw bed on earth
where your pour upon me like gasoline
until the planting season is over
and the sun strikes its match

In the Palms of Our Hands

In the fireplace flames are going down,
ashes going up.
A log husk seethes in red glow,
burning its blood, scolded
by a downdraft of cold
winter wind that dances
in our frosting breaths.

A good fire dies slowly.
Flame's wavering shadow
still ballets up the suction shaft,
ash flakes like misshapen hearts
and shadows leaving us
to worry about impalement
here by our own icicle stares.

Like ice sculptures, we pose
in our assigned spaces
while the fire whispers the same sound
as our rubbing of palms
as if to thaw their lifelines,
clear their roads that have coiled up
to strike us back now.

We somehow remember whose touch of fingers
used to spark into fireworks,
that now shatter into shivers
before the last flame slides slowly
to the underworld, sounding much
like our lips still trying to break the ice.

Mirror at the Speed of Light

The mirror moves faster than I do,
ages me ten years per day,
makes faces I've never seen,
tries to frame me
but can't decide how I should look.
I get smeared by the speed of its light.

If I play imposter and close the blinds,
it might jump to dark conclusions,
that I am solid, not a streak of gray.
If I pose in loose fits,
it can't see stretch marks on my belt,
can't see the gray alien
with light years in his eyes.

The mirror clock runs backward.
Its hands don't shake like mine;
but, like mine, they never come to rest.

Yet through that glassy hole,
the clock points to a point of light.
I see myself coming to myself,
even as the reflection no longer mimics
who I think I am.

Primal TV

Remote weapon aimed, I hunt
the Discovery Channel, my easy chair.
Raindrops by millions blow against
my perfect picture window
like an ancient swelling tribe,
a ghost nation chanting, tapping bongo.
My eyes cloud over in black and white:
Watercolor faces run down
the big screen, smear and drown
to mimes with fuzzy lips, synchless
silent screams, as if they too have heard
the dead splashing back through time,
hunters hurling spears of pure water
popping our ticking but shallow hearts.

The power goes off like a low-rated sitcom
or an artificial God of light.
The big picture condenses, squeezes in;
its glass eye closes to a fading split.
The roof caves in on my radioactive fall asleep
under the critical mass of my ancestors
who wash away the soap opera
and the easy test pattern of my life.

Why I Bought a Truck

Because it holds something,
carries the weight,
the insulation and blocks of a renovated house
that does not cast your shadow.
Shifts.
It parks in your spot.

Because it does not mire
in slinging mud,
gets a grip.
Works.
It still gets dirty.

Because it is driven,
not driven away,
not breaking down with a lonely load.
Tough.
It delivers.

Men

To be fine engines
we must pack high compression.
If our firing order is good,
no smoke will be visible from our exhausts.
Our roars are well oiled;
we drink a lot of gas,
do such hard driving
on steel-belted radials,
running over radicals,
tanking up in the red light district
at Ethyl's pump.

After a few miles,
we polish dents and cracked paint.
Our rust is easily rubbed raw.
We want our women warm as radiators,
want them to sit on our stick shifts,
want them to take a back seat
when it's time to shift into high.

Long ago kicked in the head by horsepower,
we souped up our pedal cars at an early age,
kept them well tuned,
left black marks on the roads:
the only maps we needed.

But when they don't make our models anymore,
we hammer through the junkyards,
looking for tires that haven't gone bald,
looking for fenders and spare parts,
especially spark plugs and headlights.

The Gentleman Who Woke Up as a Goat

This morning a point had
torn my designer pillow, two holes
leaking exotic feathers.
I cleaned this improper room with my eyes,
my shadow on the wall tall with devil's horns.

Something was eating me.
Suddenly, I had a craving
to eat a fork,
or to say yes I can
eat every label off every can,
or to eat my mother's dress
while she was in it,
or my father's shoes too big for me,
or my wife's box of feminine napkins
not good for setting proper tables.
I wanted junk food,
some old money,
wanted to eat my way down
Wall Street through another Depression.

And when my empire is down
to the last sweet splinter,
I'll spit it out like pieces of puzzle
for the wind to spend as it will,
then ram my head
through my neighbor's wall
and ask him
if he's eaten yet.

Going-Away Party

As I peck at my last supper,
impatient eyes already drag away the empty seats.
Behind my back I hear a vacuum removing any trace.

Determined to finish the job, I tear
at the tough flesh on my banquet plate,
pretend I am eating alive my young replacement,
whose boxes of pictures, paper clips, and diplomas
await orders outside my empty office door.

I slowly break bread into pieces of my life,
sip a wine from a bad year,
sip another that hasn't aged enough.
Like a death-row inmate, I try to make my warden wait,
my boss waiting to reward me with vibrating easy chair
and gold watch that will not keep time where I want it.

Slaps on the back sting harder and harder,
like a judge's emphatic gavel.

By midnight I've had my fill, say goodnight.

Their keys sounding like jingle bells,
they escort me to the end of the hall.
Behind my back the switch is pulled.

Sculpting the Desert

I come to the line in the sand
drawn by a serpent's shadow:
A finger writing, not straight, not deep,
the birth of a canyon
that the wind might yet redraw,
might erase from having been.
It points in two directions,
though I've traveled four and some darkly—
I who would not go straight
from cradle to grave
have staggered along a crooked road,
have shed skins thin as mirages,
until the tangle of myself
has pulled me here, has tied me here.

You've somehow arrived here too,
strangely without clothes or baggage,
without worry of stepping over the line.
Even in desert sun no scales crack through
your skin of almost pure light.
Your tracks do not hurry around themselves
like a twisted puzzle.
Here then is your starting line
and my ending.

Part 4.
Go the Way of Land

Sanctuary

Beside the road
someone has left a lantern.
Small footprints circle it
and then off.
The house through the woods is full of light.
If one wants to warm his hands
he must learn a stranger's story,
of someone who waited here for a word,
then gave up the road to absence.

One could follow through a field of wheat,
parted where the lantern and the light
from her window meet,
could watch his own dust finally settle down
in her bright and private room.

But not he who loves a road,
however dark.

Rock Road

—a wish for Susan

It's not a public road
you take to the promised land.
It's the road you build ahead of yourself
and drag behind you,
stone by sharp stone,
blister by sweating blister
beneath the sun you follow down.

You'll meet no traffic coming back.
You'll feel alone near your birthday
until you've placed the last stone
at the edge, at the dead end,
at the last sign of earth,
where the skin cools into puddles of light
and the road named for you
pours like water into your own heaven.

Duality

No sun this Sunday.
Just fog along the walkway near the church
where Sunday suits and silk dresses
line up to go to Heaven, led by the sermon
of he who was given the sign.

I limp by in last week's jeans
stained as my face,
carrying my paid-for house on my back.

Their double doors are open
but quickly close behind.
Question marks in the pews straighten
like bulbs stretching to the stained glass light
away from my shadow.

I push on in fog between light and dark,
between houses warmed with fire,
along streets lit with halos,
looking for a sign, a detour
around another dead end.

Motions

Tonight our silences walk together
in a cold slow motion
on the same abandoned road
where cricket mantras have replaced
ice clicks under logging wheels.

We go through the motions
toward thinner darkness,
our footprints deep in the road
our walks wear down.

Our feet obey the eyes navigating
a tunnel of trees bent over
a trail of ruts and holes
that could break a leg,
though we now know how to avoid a void,

we who once tried to fill the rifts
with laughing children,
with magic acts,
with house plans drawn in the dark.

Now ahead comes that distant window,
its warm hands of light
leaking out of the blinds
to touch our arrival.
But we're too like the cold we've come from,

a draft we name and drag in
to haunt the house,
an old wind to blow us further apart,
were we not both moths afloat
on yellow ropes of ghostlight.

We prefer to drift apart in place
or orbit in the dark and comfort
of familiar pain, where ages hence
we may not remember our names, our lives—
if we ever truly had them—
only see how the light from our eyes ties together,
showing the way home somehow once again.

Regret

We are always dreaming our way back,
looking behind us to see the road
rolling up like a sleeping bag,
how the trees bend over it
as if they were trying to cover up where we've been.
Suddenly we feel our pulse rise like a flame,
the dust a red fire behind us.

The past burns slowly.
Its face is red.
Its gown is ash.
Cinders float from our backs and seem like travelers,
not gray husks so slowly falling down.

The Last Supper Date

on a one-way road
in the warm heart of Paradise
is a red light
where the road
dead ends

has no turns
or turnarounds
though the bulbs
bloom seasons of
green yellow red
and roadside roses
stir in breezes that once
were perfect angel breaths
with no borders to hold them in

I get out to pick the perfect one
but its petals blacken
into cold pieces of night
on which my teeth chatter
shatter at a sin-eater's last meal

from inside a closed flower shop
I hear God trying to hold it in

Direction

The night blooms
tilt hopefully to the east.
I too turn to look over my shoulder,
looking for moving light
when the night I have bumped
and dreamed beneath
has turned inside out to the other side.

A red bubble lifts up
behind me like an ancient prayer,
erupts and passes me by,
burns a trail up my back
that turns dark and misleading.

I cross, re-cross the four lost winds
pace back and forth between opposite poles,
between dusk and dawn
like so many travelers
who know more of their going than of their where.

Road Steam

Along the steaming road
the stones are beginning to pop.
The sky is a dripping wax.
Tall tree stumps smoke like chimneys.
My feet stick to the main road
just as slugs stick to tombstones.
Rubbing off on me, slime comes forth as moral.

But this morning, the roadworkers keep pointing,
saying this is the highway to heaven.

Ahead a black cloud of flies approaches like rain.

Daydreaming at Rush Hour

I fancy the red light is that rose
I've been told to stop and smell.
In the wind the bulb sways back and forth,
leaving a bloody streak on the sky,
a kind of rainbow after storms of wrecks.
Blue streaks keep passing me by:
smears on a street dead at both ends.
But in slow motion the red light of the rose wilts.
Something green blooms.
I press down on the pedal and spring.

Miniverse, My Universe

An overworked metaphor,
I drive home to Unity,
where only naps travel far,
where maps are used to swat the local flies.
Too heavy for my shock absorbers,
I steer obliquely now,
veer and smear thinly
along a road dead at both ends.

Still, the small stem
of my mind snaps,
flies off on a wild loose chase,
and still my deep-space probe
does not penetrate the flickers
of brighter stars.
I burn out among the pin pricks
of light, only remember
the vision of your touch,
not the common fuel of light years
that stretched your fingers toward mine
like comets curving or toll roads
paving their own way,

and how like roads
they tangle and turn away,
get lost
in their smaller selves.

Into Some Deeper Night

Into some deeper night
the train whistle warns
of our crossing.
No tracks in gravel,
our soles crush
the next moment;
our blisters
replay the last.
We hitch our eyes
to distance, pause
at the deafening rhythm
of steel on cross ties
fading from earshot
like dying rain,

and we go to embrace
the last silence that we heard.

Earthen Well

Even the stars seem burned out, greenly ill.
Desert roads fall into a filling well
where streams choke on brontosaurus bones
brittle as dust, as history.

Beyond tunnel vision, the eye of a needle opens:
Serpent jaws crack the bad egg of me.
In a new solution I'm light liquid now,
my weight on new scales barely shifting the tides,
even as I harden into fossil stone,
the heart ground down into meal.

Above my extinction the surface eye clearing
where mockingbirds flutter in the spring bath,
whistling a greening song to wiggling road:
a lure from the whole we're in.
For them, too, the cobra's jaws grind,
hissing a song of bone and feather.

Somehow higher than we, the pecking orders
fall from hunger, we from greed.
Our common mother Earth gangrened, a sick Medusa,
her coiled roads, rivers, lightning,
nerves on end
are ready to strike, digest, reclaim,
restitch her cloudy body gown:
the bloody rags, the vital organs.

Ice Steeples, Road Signs

From light years apart the stars sleet
down into the same wet blanket of ice,
a jagged indifference, a global cube, a crack in the safe,
all-night snaps and spiritual shudders of earthly things.

The power goes off;
I am left with cold logic
and a hearth of lowering flames.
The North Star blossoms into frost,
now the sign to leave, not to follow.
Our numb helping hands
touch across radio waves;
our fingers break like bridges.
The weak channel crackles,
echoes of ghosts and snapping pines.
Weather prophets issue traveler's warnings:
accidents, signs of ducks frozen to the lake,
bucks locked on the horns of dilemma,
olive branches shattering like glass.

Tonight I chip away the cold pieces of myself,
watch the fallen stars wink briefly
from their ancient hearts,
their white fires freezing in
touch with earth.

I go back inside, await artificial light.
The smoky fire I breathed back to life
goes up in cloud,
falls back as ice:
stalagmite beds or nails to dream on,
to feel their points search inside me
for a warmer way.

Part 5.
Go the Way of Water

Progress

In the right frame of my window
the ducks party in the lake;
stage left the backhoe digs a foundation,
eats the earth that holds it up.
The arias of diesel stack and throat horn harmonize
across a field of goats, the only grazers natural
in soft or metal blades of grass.

The ducks fish now below the surface;
the digger disappears in its own hole.

A vulture bends a patient limb, waits
like a word hard to say
for the machine to bury itself,
for a daffy duck to wade into nets
and broadcast waves of bullseye,
so that nothing pronounced dead
goes to waste.

River Pulse

smoothed by wear
in any panned stream is a load of stones

call them eggs that never hatched

call one a heart too hard to break
that keeps the river flowing

Lighthouse

deep in its own mouth
the night river carves two shores

fog horns and cattle wail for a clearer coast
and home reaches out its ancient arm
a tunnel a deep well of water and light

a tomb a cradle
a passage to either side

Cottonmouth Catchers in a Night Swamp

The trick is to charm its bobbing head with light.
Make the devil stare till he's blind,
and while your flimsy lifeboat crawls toward the other bank,
let your own arm become a snake,
coil back with your right hand open
like a pure mouth capable of swallowing
something bigger than itself.

Let your arm strike as a strangler,
clamp the serpent just below the head,
cram this ancient sinner in a bag.

Now row back to sunrise,
milk him for all he's worth,
keep him charmed with living light,
never showing him your shadow,
your black spot,
your bullseye.

The Underground River

On its back is a plugged farmer's well
where his girls chattered and sang,
let down their long ropes of hair,
drawing up the most vocal water.

An indoor faucet plugs, unplugs city water now.
The world comes in metered from remote.
The TV chatters; the girls are on mute.
Father falls asleep to the mantra of microwave.
The family garden grows in the nearby Wal-Mart.

Mother, had she seen the currents and circuits connecting,
would likely have pulled the plug, fallen into the well's
deep journey, not into the bone-cold ground near the house
where birds drink the dewdrops on her headstone
as if to drink her purest tears,
while ghosts of rainwater rust in nearby barrels.

The girls only date cable repairmen, mechanics,
and plumbers, those who have the tools
to tighten the leaking and the loose,
to keep everything running in place.
There are no more animals to feed, save themselves.
Every year the birds know fewer songs.

Under a remodeled house and its softer beds,
the underground river quenches the dead
but sweats the dreams of those who live in wires.
Still carrying a tune, still carving out its future,
the river beneath is always beginning, always arriving,
its headwaters, its mouth full of the same eternal song,
lyrics of a language they no longer understand,
a gurgle or a death rattle now in their plugged and distant ears.

Dream of the Electric Eel

nothing shocks me
not even the black leaves forming the sky
of this swamp nor my shape
in the dark water dammed with ash

no one to hug me
I am my own arm
have made the absence of touch a weapon
made my voice an image in the current
too late announcing my coming

fishermen throw me back without touching the line
snakes shed a skin of ash
when I grow suddenly warm

underwater lightning
I have left a trail of fire
on the river's back
for mine is the voice that boils water
yet makes it feel cold

they say an eel is lower than a snake
that even the swamp is above him
but I say I have fallen like a power
line leaping on the river
that when I go down
all I touch twitches
and rises to the top

Knots

How many waves my voyage makes
is known only to the shores.
There island boys cast their lines,
hoping to catch news
of the deeper world,
not to hook the surface ships
whose names are too far to read,
whose captains wear the spray of cold waters,
who map rocks cutting through the waves
to a beach where only their eyes land
like a blank message in a bottle.

Tonight on my floating island,
my drifting hull with smokestacks for trees,
I am too weary from storm to sail away.
I drop the anchor like a dead bird,
watch a forbidden coastline bob up and down.

Island girls wave to me from home fires.
I warm my hands on their distant light,
briefly touched by their story.
Know we all are passing ships,
self-tangled anglers
watching drift off
the one that got away.

The Treasure of Bone

we hunters follow the river
swarm silently in a hive of nerves
and keep the feet a moving target
we've heard the tone of a bloodhound soar
when the diamondback pierced his foot
seen how he snapped off its head
assuming that victory has no poison
and limped into the tense undergrowth
ahead of the sickness on his heels

how many falls and crossings later
we lame and swollen
come upon him
and rearrange his bones
among the hollow stalks
and wonder at the miracle
of how flesh disappears
only to feed an earth
dressed in the jewelry of bone

The Hunted River

Dream that somewhere,
maybe in another universe,
a river runs forever wild,
purified by its own voyage.
Yet, at its calmer moments the animals drink.

It ain't sportin' but shoot 'em in their beds if you find 'em, my father
orders.

My father teaches me how to hunt
along this river he says is deep enough for any man,
and I begin to think of how it swells
with rain and floods with fertile soil my father's land,
harvested by hand and then by gun.

*Boy, pay attention! Stop carryin' that gun like a rattlesnake. If y' wanna
bag yore limit, git that barrel into position. You ain't gonna learn how t'
do this in any of them books you read.*

Still they listen, these ears, to water on the run,
wondering if it could change its course.
It seems a road I could walk on,
a current to take this gun to another world
to rust as relic of forgotten ways.

My father is smart.
He, too, follows the river.
He knows rabbits have to drink.
They are drinking my water, he's complained.
Never hunt on another man's land, he's advised.
Never trespass on dreams that can't come true, I hear.

*Boy, we ain't shootin' stars! Git that gun pointed down to earth. But
maybe it don't matter none. Sissy as you are, a rabbit'd probably think*

yore barrel's a carrot. Maybe you oughta put on a skirt, go stand in the
garden and be a scarecrow. They ain't no good fer nuthin' anyway.

The other side of the river could be another world.
Maybe there a transparent moon swells from a river bubble
out of range of archers and snipers
aiming to hear it explode.

Damn near 18 years old and still skinny! Boy, when y' gonna grow some?
You wouldn't make a good meal for a grasshopper. Around these parts a
poor man's gotta kill to eat. Gotta get some meat on yore bones, or I cain't
even call you son.

I've practiced scaring rats and shooting cans,
comforted that metal does not twitch in death throes.
My father wonders why I miss so much,
why my aim is high,
why I've wasted so much ammunition.

Lookie yonder! Cock yore gun, boy. We got visitors.

Across the meadow in rank and file waits
a pack of wild dogs, former best friends perhaps
of men who didn't feed them.
Their leader is black but for the bullseye on his chest.
His hair is curled with burs, is ragged
from barb-wire fences and the teeth of challengers.
As if in a cage, he paces back and forth, all nose
twitching, reading the silence and scents.

He watches our nervous barrels, remembers
the bite of buckshot, folds himself into a small target
and howls as if to say *I'll find a man without a gun.*
Then he leads his hungry pack off, into dark woods,
watching over his long back for mistakes, for fear.

For a moment eighteen eyes in the shadows blink,
then swivel and disappear.

Whew, that wuz close! See now why a man oughta never be without a
gun? Any man's a meal if he's outnumbered.

I nod my head but wonder if I could even point
the barrel down a mouth that would eat me,
though I feel my father's red river surging through my veins.
His blood, however rich and ancient, drowns me.
Life tastes like blood, he's boomed.

Boy, y' walk like a pregnant woman! Pick up yore feet and put 'em down
like y' mean to go somewhere.

It's a snap to hear the hunter coming.
Twigs and dry branches crack under our weight,
bones breaking in the ears of frightened animals.
Men do not smell themselves,
but deer noses and long barrels
for a moment split the wind, then a gust
as one breathes in, the other out.

This here rifle's been worth the price. A man's the only critter that don't
have to git close to kill.

I look up then to a buzzard above,
reflect on it as a noble life
that eats death but does not kill.

A minor to now, I've only been death's pallbearer.
Always my father has sent me ahead
to hand the dead to my mother, the stained artist,
whose knife resculpts the corpses,
whose hands baptize them in the purest river water
so they are clean enough for my plate.

Cleaning, my father then yawns, *is woman's work.*
But I too wish to wash my hands, soap everything.

A bubble in my heart pops: a flinch!
Near the river, snow white and silent.
I am the only hunter in the world who sees it.
It has stopped making noise on its carrot, lies stiff in its bed.
My father's eyes have crossed the open field,
do not notice how I could extend my arms with this barrel
and touch life, feel its breathing move me up and down.

As if standing in a storm's eye where every breath
gathers to pause so deeply in the heart of fear,
old hunters can smell silence.
A great void in the ears swivels my father's eyes.
He looks back like a whisper, traces the path of my eyes.
Too late I look away.

*Easy now. Our supper's waitin'. Y' 'member what I taught you? Hold the
barrel steady and squeeze the trigger real gentle like. Right between the
eyes. Won't hurt him none. Better do it 'fore he runs. Now, take a deep
breath and lower yore sights. It's time.*

Wind, river, and blood pause,
stalled by a dam thicker than courage,
then all begin to whisper like an audience.
I imagine the river a snake coiling up;
the wind breathes heavier, parting the stems
of grass in the rabbit's bed, giving me, if I will, the clearest
of shots. My veins bulge out like barrels; a touched nerve
curls my unwilling finger, bends my sights
to a small thumping heart.

Father? I softly pray.

It's all right, son. It's what we gotta do.

Passing Through

when I became the river
the wet feet kept walking
no longer wondering where
became stones tumbled smooth

going was no longer downhill or falling
in eternal nightfall
where the dead end stories
they never could begin

but then I heard my river's voice
sometimes a whisper sometimes a roar
that rose far above the rocky falls

and then I saw I am the eye
in any night sky
a telescope of vision
that sees everywhere at once

and I smelled the gun gusts of history
that blew me upward
and I flew through the wildfires
through the deep earth tunnels
leading out the other side

I touched the white head of Everest
where gravity seemed to float
and I tasted the starlight
frozen for centuries of secrets

when the thin skin shed from me
when the heart became pure water
and waved through the ages

I became the pure touch of wind
I became everything it touches
everywhere it blows
everything it knows

Part 6.
Go the Way of Wind

The Wind Is Often Sudden Here

The fan chokes on air thick as walls.
Suddenly the storm door blows open.
Shadows and leaves dance in.
Your long, dark hair flies at half mast.
My carefully signed documents and deeds
lift off with the leaves
rattling, fluttering
through the shattered window.
There the loud wind pins leaflets,
wills, and final notices to the stone wall,

their death rattles deafening now
in the same wind, the same breath
that once blew a kiss.

Weeding the National Harvest

A cloud comes over moonface
and a cold mist dusts our forbidden crops.
Water stars twinkle on the squash leaves
when the full moon removes its cloud mask.

A storm is shoving into place,
imposing its dark moodscapes,
its loud cannons, its stormtrooper winds.

A bolt chops down the apple tree,
and the garden flashes black and white.
A crossfire of seeds rips through
the slumping scarecrow's heart,
shreds the colorful crops into long black snakes,
into dark food for thought.

Nearing is the rumble of a deeper wave.
In the calm before, the scarred moon
aims its beams along the ruins of garden rows.
Dust swarms within their tubes
like confused rain, like the fear
we have now for our land.

The Last Saint of the Empire

Stranger, I am cupping in my hands
the land's last water for you.
You will not drink alone.
The sun too is steaming in this meager pool.

Drink before the water boils away.

What you have won is mostly smoke:
Above us, old mystics, old clouds,
redden from the dust of battle:
the wind twists them like sponges,
wringing out across the valley
a dry and crimson rain:
Even the gentle, holy winds rub
together like flint:
below them the frocks flame:
the shadows of monks are dark ash
piling up in prayer.

My invader, my wounded heir,
you are drinking my boiling blood.
You must swallow what you conquer.
You must dress for the weather you bring.

It is a hot day:
Smell the feathers of the angels burning.

Faith

Somehow the balance that keeps
the empty winter trees from falling
keeps me standing still.

The closest neighbors move away, seem dead.
A greater wind carries away my wife.
The leaves still blow in their direction.
They all left their shadows behind;
in window light their stems still leaf
through a black and white film on my walls.

I sleep with an oak pillow on my head,
but somehow the dream breaks through
these roots of my wooden days
when I alone cannot leave.

Somehow the tree leans back
against the wind
that sails its many leaves.

Windfall

To know the fate of winds
is to dance together in the eye of a storm,
inhale, exhale, hold
the breath to its dying
and on a purer shore
somehow stir again,

flicker from a lighthouse candle,
the soul focused in the eye of a needle
that probes beyond the pain.
There is the nanosecond of arrival home
and there the leaving;
there the windsong forever circles,
blows open our eyes
only to shut again.

Or might true voice sigh once, true vision
give light to stars that have no need,
as all join in a sad perfection
and never sing again.

How Trees Travel

old trees guard the road
waiting for feathers
waiting for songs to fill them
so that travelers
are not alone in their own music

it is a truth of trees:
the bigger they are
the closer they have grown to one another
along this road their long travelled root
a great finger pointing the way
for their children the birds
who are now bright leaves
chattering south
who have left
the hollow trunks to fall

Relativity

The highest achievement of my relatives
is blood pressure. Like them, my window
on the windy world tenses and cracks
into a small river with a big mouth,
ribbed with minor tributaries,
serious wounds now freezing silent.
Like them, my mind freezes under the pressure
of tunnel vision and black mindholes.

As here, cold fogs Einstein's pane
like a prayer answered in riddle,
but shifts the light,
beyond a memory prism,
beyond any prophecy or calculation,
beyond the power of any river dammed.

It's the icy finger that fits all,
seems our own but sewn to a greater hand,
a probe at once from then and now
that leaves its print, its point
on the shiver of dunce and genius alike.

A wind frozen into slow motion,
all angles take its shape,
piled like brittle leaves against foundations,
holes blown in steel theories,
fools made savant beyond their small equations—
of hope equals cope, truth equals law—
all dressed in gowns of ancient unborn light.

We inhale but once this cosmic dust,
a common sense unlike knowledge:
A window shatters into stars,
fading in the empty frame,
small, light pieces of the puzzle.

Acknowledgments

Grateful acknowledgements are made to the following publications in which many of these poems first appeared (sometimes in earlier versions):

Black Bear Review: "The Gentleman Who Woke Up as a Goat," "Primal TV"
The Bridge: "Lighthouse" Chants: "The Treasure of Bone"
The Chattahoochee Review: "Men"
Dancing Shadows Review: "The Meaning of Dogs"
En Passant: "The Last Saint of the Empire"
ELF (Eclectic Literary Forum): "The New World Dictionary," "River Pulse"
Foundling Review: "Knots"
Gaia: A Journal of Literary & Environmental Arts: "What Missing the Cat Means," "Veterans Know a Purr Is Just an Infant Growl"
The Grasslands Review: "The Glass Heart"
Green Hills Literary Lantern: "Progress"
The Habersham Review: "Regret"
Hammers: "Why I Bought a Truck"
Hudson Valley Echoes: "Wanting to Write Songs"
Innisfree: "Fading Pictures," "Duality"
Iodine Poetry Journal: "Daydreaming at Rush Hour"
Literary Fragments: "Faith"
The Lucid Stone: "Windfall"
The Lullwater Review: "Prophets Climbing to Machu Picchu"
Main Street Rag: "The Wind Is Often Sudden Here"
Midwest Quarterly: "Treasure Hunt"
Negative Capability: "The Juggler Tells His Children of Dreams"
Neonbeam (U.K.): "Motions"
Opus Literary Magazine: "Punctuation"
Permafrost: "Sanctuary"
Pinyon Poetry: "The Scarecrow at Harvest Time"
Plainsongs: "Miniverse, My Universe"

Poems That Thump in the Dark: "Relativity"
The Purple Monkey: "Direction"
Rain Dog Review: "Road Steam"
Remark Poetry: "Going Through the Motions"
River Poets Journal: "The Last Supper Date"
Southern Poetry Review: "Dream of the Electric Eel"
The Sow's Ear: "Confessions of the Slower Sprinter"
Spoon River Poetry Review: "The Light Sedative of Dark,"
    "Earthen Well"
The Stickman Review: "Ice Steeples, Road Signs," "Rock Road,"
    "How Trees Travel"
Wind: "Into Some Deeper Night"
Writers' Forum: "Cottonmouth Catchers in a Night Swamp"
Xanadu: "Ice-Sparkles"

The author extends special thanks to Shared Roads Press, now defunct, for publishing the first edition of *The Hunted River* and giving FutureCycle Press the rights to the second edition.

Cover and book design by Diane Kistner (dkistner@futurecycle.org); photo of river and trees in autumn by AquaColor; Vietnam-era barracks photo of the author by a Navy buddy whose name he can no longer remember; "now" photo of the author by Diane Kistner; all text and titling, Adobe Garamond Pro.

BOOKS AND CHAPBOOKS BY ROBERT S. KING

When Stars Fall Down as Snow
Dream of the Electric Eel
The Traveller's Tale
The Hunted River
The Gravedigger's Roots

The author maintains a personal website at www.robertsking.com. There you will find samples of his writing, blog, calendar, and links to reviews of his work.

About FutureCycle Press

FutureCycle Press is dedicated to publishing lasting English-language poetry and flash fiction books, chapbooks, and anthologies in both print-on-demand and ebook formats. Founded in 2007 by long-time independent editor/publishers and partners Diane Kistner and Robert S. King, the press incorporated as a nonprofit in 2012. A number of our editors are distinguished poets and authors in their own right, and we have been actively involved in the small press movement going back to the early seventies.

Our annual anthology, *FutureCycle*, combines poetry and flash fiction. The FutureCycle Poetry Book Prize and honorarium is awarded annually for the best full-length volume of poetry we publish in a calendar year. We are dedicated to giving all authors we publish the care their work deserves, making our catalog of titles the most distinguished it can be, and paying forward any earnings to fund more great books.

We've learned a few things about independent publishing over the years. We've also evolved a unique, resilient publishing model that allows us to focus mainly on vetting and preserving for posterity the most books of exceptional quality without becoming overwhelmed with bookkeeping and mailing, fundraising activities, or taxing editorial and production "bubbles." To find out more about what we are doing, come see us at www.futurecycle.org.

www.ingramcontent.com/pod-product-compliance
Lightning Source LLC
Chambersburg PA
CBHW070041110426
42741CB00036B/3126